BIG ANIMALS

Contents

Elephant

ANIMALS

written by Mary Gribbin
illustrated by Peter Bull

Words in **bold** are explained
in the glossary.

Ladybird books are widely available, but in case of
difficulty may be ordered by post or telephone from:

Ladybird Books – Cash Sales Department
Littlegate Road Paignton Devon TQ3 3BE
Telephone 01803 554761

A catalogue record for this book is available
from the British Library

Published by Ladybird Books Ltd Loughborough Leicestershire UK
Ladybird Books Inc Auburn Maine 04210 USA

African elephants are the largest and heaviest of all land animals. They live in groups called **herds**, with the females looking after the **calves**.

Elephants feed on leaves, bark and plants. Elephants drink more than 80 litres of water a day, which is as much as 140 pints of milk. Elephants' long tusks are really overgrown teeth. These can be over three metres long – taller than an adult person.

Elephants pull down branches with their long trunks.

Elephants also use their trunks to breathe, drink and shower themselves.

Elephants can pick things up with their trunks, too.

Polar Bear

Polar bears live in the **Arctic**, where the sea is often covered by ice. Big paws help polar bears to run, jump and swim. Polar bears also have sharp claws which help them to climb up slippery slopes. Polar

bears' white fur means that they cannot be seen easily in this snowy land. This helps the bears to catch their **prey**. Polar bears have a thick layer of fat beneath their skin, and a thick fur coat to keep them warm.

Polar bears have fur on the bottom of their feet to stop them slipping on the ice.

Seals and fish are favourite food for polar bears.

Polar bears wait by ice holes to catch seals coming up to breathe.

Anaconda Snake

Anaconda snakes are the largest snakes in the world. They can swim well and often live near water, in the hot, wet rain forests of South America. Anacondas belong to a group of snakes called **boas**. Adult anacondas hunt fish and large animals. They even catch turtles and **caimans**.

Anacondas wait patiently for prey to come along.

Anacondas strike quickly by coiling themselves round the animal, squeezing it tightly.

Anacondas open their jaws very wide and swallow their meal, whole.

Gorilla

Gorillas wake at dawn.

They spend a lot of the day eating, resting and grooming each other.

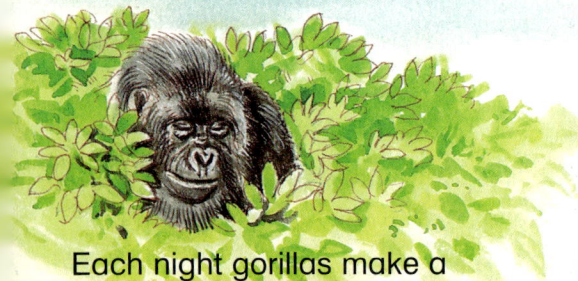

Each night gorillas make a new nest to sleep in.

Gorillas are a kind of animal called an **ape**, and they are closely related to us. Apes live in family groups in the forests of Central Africa. Young gorillas climb trees. Adult gorillas normally walk on the ground, using their hands and feet.

Gorillas also use their hands to pick food. They like to eat green leaves and fruit. Older male gorillas have silver rather than black hair on their backs.

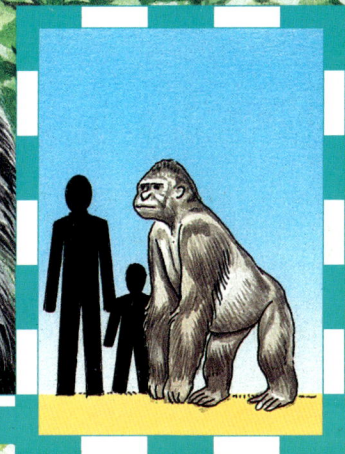

Giraffe

The open grasslands of Africa are the giraffes' home. Giraffes are the world's tallest animals. The big bones in giraffes' necks make these animals so tall. Giraffes eat leaves and shoots which are out of reach of any other animals.

Giraffes may fight, or wrestle, with each other, using their necks. Young giraffes may be attacked by lions, but even young giraffes can run fast to escape.

Giraffes wrap their long tongues round a branch and strip off all the leaves.

To drink, giraffes bend their necks slowly. Giraffes are careful not to lose their balance.

Giraffes spread their front legs wide and lower their necks down to the water.

Hippopotamus

Hippos live in Africa. They spend much of the day in rivers or lakes, hiding from the fierce Sun. At night, when it is cooler,

hippos come out onto land. Here they eat plants, especially grasses that grow near water. Baby hippos are often born on land.

Hippos look large and clumsy, but they are very good swimmers.

Hippos can dive underwater and even walk on the bottom of a river or lake.

When hippos are resting, their ears, eyes and nostrils appear above the water.

15

Tiger

Tigers are the largest cats in the world. They are also the only wild cats to have a striped coat, which helps to give them **camouflage**.

Tigers live in Asia. Some tigers prefer the hot rain forests there, but other tigers live where there is deep snow in winter. Tigers can swim well, but they do not climb trees.

Tigers hunt alone, often at night. They track down deer and cattle for food.

Tigers hide in tall grass and creep up on prey very quietly.

Tigers leap out and pounce on their prey, taking the animal by surprise.

Crocodile

Crocodiles lived on the Earth at the same time as dinosaurs. A crocodile's skin is as tough as armour. It is covered with **scales** that fit together well, so that the crocodile can move easily. Crocodiles often lurk in shallow water, waiting to catch their food.

Baby crocodiles **hatch** out from eggs that the mother lays in a nest.

As soon as baby crocodiles have hatched, they head straight for the water.

Sometimes the mother carries the babies to the water in her mouth.

Crocodiles' eyes and nostrils are almost on top of their heads. This helps crocodiles to see and breathe while the rest of their body is underwater. When an animal comes to drink, the crocodile rushes out of the water and drags the animal back underwater.

Kangaroo

Kangaroos belong to a group of mammals called **marsupials**. Kangaroos live mainly in Australia. They have very powerful back legs. Kangaroos move by using their powerful legs to hop and jump. A baby kangaroo spends the early months of its life inside the **pouch** at the front of its mother's body.
Kangaroos eat plants.

Baby kangaroos are called **joeys**.

Joeys live in their mother's pouch, where they feed on milk.

Young kangaroos first leave the pouch when they are about six months old.

Fascinating Facts

Elephant

An elephant's trunk is made from its top lip and nose, which are joined together.

Polar Bear

A polar bear can stay underwater for two minutes, without air.

Anaconda Snake

The anaconda snake can grow to nearly ten metres in length, which is as long as a coach.

Gorilla

Gorillas talk to each other, using twenty-two different sounds.

Giraffe

A giraffe's heart weighs eleven kilograms, which is heavier than a small dog. This large heart pumps blood up the giraffe's long neck to the brain.

Hippopotamus

A small type of hippopotamus called the pygmy hippo, lives in the rain forests of West Africa.

Tiger

It takes a year before a young tiger is able to hunt on its own. Until then the mother catches food for her youngsters. A tiger has a very large appetite, and can eat the equivalent of thirty whole chickens a day.

Crocodile

Most crocodiles live in rivers, but the saltwater crocodile can also swim in the sea.

Kangaroo

The red kangaroo grows to about two metres tall, which is taller than most people.

Glossary

Ape A mammal which is our closest relative in the animal kingdom.

Arctic The frozen, northern part of the world which includes the North Pole.

Boa A type of snake which lives in Central and South America.

Caiman A small type of crocodile living in Central and South America. Unfortunately, its skin is sometimes made into clothes, boots and bags.

Calf A name used for several types of young animal. These include elephants and cows.

Camouflage The way in which an animal can hide from other animals, using its markings or body shape.

Hatch When an animal breaks out of an egg.

Herd Animals which live together, often in family groups, and which feed on plants.

Joey The Australian name given to a baby kangaroo.

Marsupial A mammal which spends its early life in a pouch at the front of its mother's body.

Pouch A fold of skin, like a pocket on an apron. Young marsupials live in a pouch after being born.

Prey An animal which is eaten by other animals.

Scales A tough covering which protects the body of reptiles and fish. Some scales, like those on crocodiles, are bony.

Index

Comparative sizes

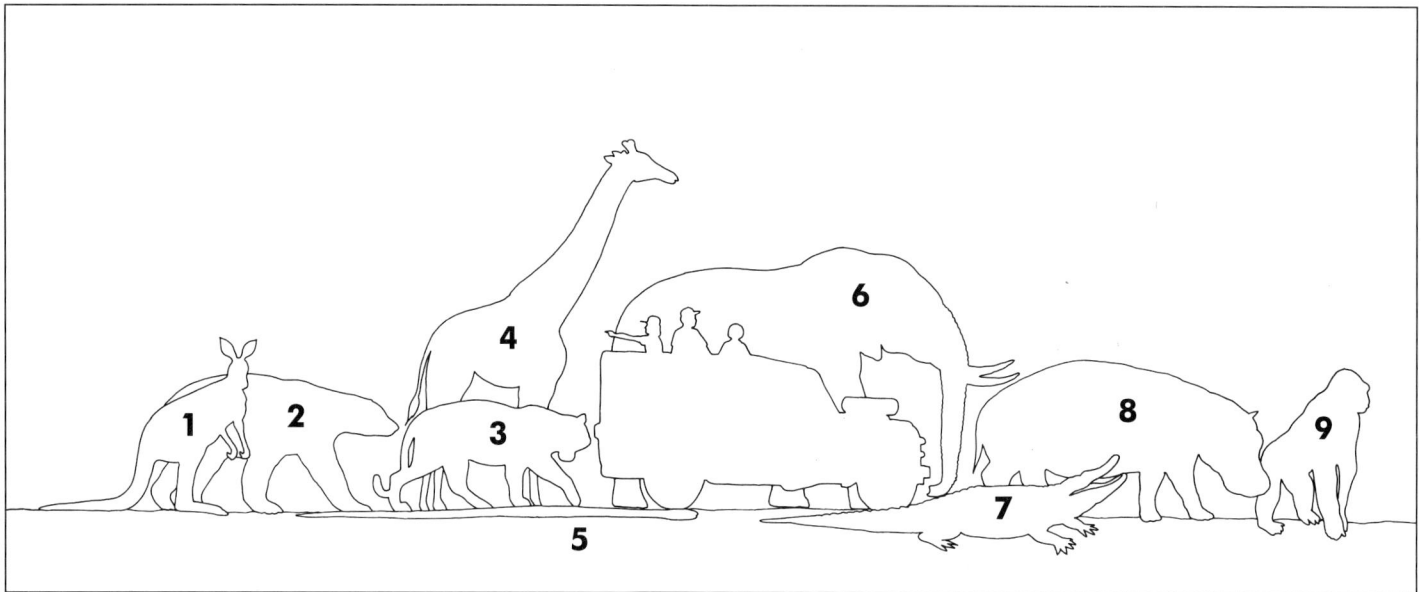

1 Kangaroo

Kangaroos are the biggest marsupials. Adult kangaroos grow to be taller than a grown-up.

2 Polar Bear

Polar bears are the biggest meat-eating land animals. The biggest polar bear ever known weighed 1,000 kilograms, which is as much as a family car.

3 Tiger

The Siberian tiger is the largest of all tigers. Tigers have been known to even attack elephants.

4 Giraffe

Giraffes have very long tongues. Giraffes' tongues can be as long as 40 centimetres, which is the length of a child's arm.

5 Anaconda Snake

Anacondas can open their jaws wide enough to swallow small crocodiles, whole.

6 Elephant

African elephants are much taller, and have bigger ears and tusks, than Asian elephants.

7 Crocodile

The saltwater crocodile and the Nile crocodile are the largest of all crocodiles.

8 Hippopotamus

Hippos have the largest mouths of all mammals that live on land.

9 Gorilla

Gorillas are the biggest of all the apes. Male gorillas can be taller than a grown-up.

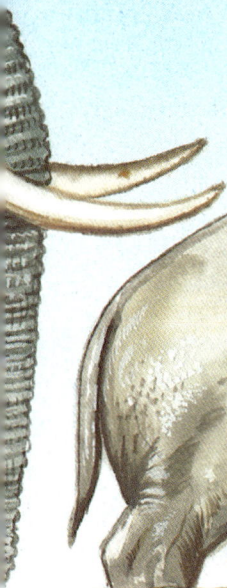